MW01288906

Knock Knock!

Funny Knock Knock Jokes for Kids

Johnny B.Laughing

"The Joke King"

DEDICATION

This book is dedicated to the one's out there that love to be silly, have fun, and laugh. It's because of humor that the world keeps spinning..

KNOCK KNOCK JOKES

Knock knock!
Who's there?
Adore!
Adore who?
Adore stands between us, open up!

Knock knock!
Who's there?
Underwear!
Underwear who?
Underwear my baby is tonight?

Knock knock!
Who's there?
Banana!
Banana who?
Banana split so ice creamed!

Knock knock!
Who's there?
Abbey!
Abbey who?
Abbey stung me on the nose!

Knock knock!
Who's there?
Aaron!
Aaron who?
Aaron the barber's floor!

Knock knock!
Who's there?
Baby owl!
Baby owl who?
Baby owl see you later.

Knock knock!
Who's there?
Bacon!
Bacon who?
Bacon a cake for your birthday!

Knock knock!
Who's there?
Cindy!
Cindy who?
Cindy next one in please!

Knock knock!
Who's there?
Chuck!
Chuck who?
Chuck in a sandwich for lunch!

Knock knock!
Who's there?
Bach!
Bach who?
Bach to work!

Knock knock!
Who's there?
Acid!
Acid who?
Accidently on purpose!

Knock knock!
Who's there?
Acis!
Acis who?
Acis spades!

Knock knock!
Who's there?
Ada!
Ada who?
A diamond is forever!

Knock knock!
Who's there?
Adair!
Adair who?
Adair once but now I'm bald now!

Knock knock!
Who's there?
Adam!
Adam who?
Adam up and tell me the total!

Knock knock!
Who's there?
Adelia!
Adelia who?
Adelia the cards after you cut the deck!

Knock knock!
Who's there?
Adeline!
Adeline who?
Adeline extra to the letter!

Knock knock!
Who's there?
Adolf!
Adolf who?
Adolf ball hit me in the mouth!

Knock knock!
Who's there?
Burglar!
Burglar who?
Burglars don't knock!

Knock knock!
Who's there?
Curry!
Curry who?
Curry me back home will you!?

Knock knock!
Who's there?
Curly!
Curly who?
Curly Q!

Knock knock!
Who's there?
C's!
C's who?
C's the day!

Knock knock!
Who's there?
Crock and dial!
Crock and dial who?
Crock and dial Dundee!

Knock knock!
Who's there?
Crete!
Crete who?
Crete to see you again!

Knock knock!
Who's there?
Cows!
Cows who?
Cows go moo not who!

Knock knock!
Who's there?
Cotton!
Cotton who?
Cotton a trap!

Knock knock!
Who's there?
Cod!
Cod who?
Cod red-handed!

Knock knock!
Who's there?
Comic!
Comic who?
Comic and see me sometime!

Knock knock!
Who's there?
Cologne!
Cologne who?
Cologne me names won't help!

Knock knock!
Who's there?
Closure!
Closure who?
Closure mouth when you eat!

Knock knock!
Who's there?
Claude!
Claude who?
Claude up by the cat!

Knock knock!
Who's there?
Clark!
Clark who?
Clark your car in the garage!

Knock knock!
Who's there?
Clare!
Clare who?
Clare your throat before you speak!

Knock knock!
Who's there?
A Fred!
A Fred who?
Who's a Fred of the Big Bad Wolf?

Knock knock!
Who's there?
Agatha!
Agatha who?
Agatha headache. Do you have an aspirin?

Knock knock!
Who's there?
Agent!
Agent who?
Agentle breeze!

Knock knock!
Who's there?
Ahmed!
Ahmed who?
Ahmed a big mistake coming here!

Knock knock!
Who's there?
Aladdin!
Aladdin who?
Aladdin the street wants a word with you!

Knock knock!
Who's there?
Alba!
Alba who?
Alba in the kitchen if you need me!

Knock knock!
Who's there?
Albee!
Albee who?
Albee a monkey's uncle!

Knock knock!
Who's there?
Albert!
Albert who!
Albert you don't know who this is!

Knock knock!
Who's there?
Aldo!
Aldo who?
Aldo anywhere with you!

Knock knock!
Who's there?
Costa!
Costa who?
Costa lot!

Knock knock!
Who's there?
Cook!
Cook who?
Cuckoo yourself, I don't come here to be insulted!

Knock knock!
Who's there?
Cookie!
Cookie who?
Cookie quit and now I have to make all the food!

Knock knock!
Who's there?
Cole!
Cole who?
Cole as a cucumber!

Knock knock!
Who's there?
Coffin!
Coffin who?
Coffin and spluttering!

Knock knock!
Who's there?
Coda!
Coda who?
Coda paint!

Knock knock!
Who's there?
Alec!
Alec who?
Alec-tricity. Isn't that a shock!

Knock knock!
Who's there?
Aleta!
Aleta who?
Aleta from the bill man!

Knock knock!
Who's there?
Aitch!
Aitch who?
Bless You!

Knock knock!
Who's there?
Cheese!
Cheese who?
Cheese a cute girl!

Knock knock!
Who's there?
Blue!
Blue who?
Blue away with the wind!

Knock knock!
Who's there!
Boo!
Boo who?
Why are you crying? It's just a joke!

Knock knock!
Who's there?
Iguana.
Iguana who?
Iguana go home now!

Knock knock!
Who's there?
Butter!
Butter who?
Butter wrap up because it's cold out there!

Knock knock!
Who's there?
Bean!
Bean who?
Bean working very hard all day long!

Knock knock!
Who's there?
Nobel!
Nobel who?
Nobel. Seriously that's the reason that I knocked.

Knock knock!
Who's there?
Bed!
Bed who?
Bed you will never guess who I am!

Knock knock!
Who's there?
Dewey!
Dewey who?
Dewey have to keep doing this?

Knock knock!
Who's there?
Cozi!
Cozi who?
Cozi has to!

Knock knock!
Who's there?
Cliff!
Cliff who?
Cliff hanger!

Knock knock!
Who's there?
Crispin!
Crispin who?
Crispin crunchy is how I like my cereal!

Knock knock!
Who's there?
Cork!
Cork who?
Cork and beans!

Knock knock!
Who's there?
Robin!
Robin who?
Robin from the rich and giving to the poor!

Knock knock!
Who's there?
Canoe!
Canoe who?
Canoe come out and play with me?

Knock knock!
Who's there?
Bowl!
Bowl who?
Bowl me over!

Knock knock!
Who's there?
Bossy!
Bossy who?
Bossy just fired me!

Knock knock!
Who's there?
Hand!
Hand who?
Have over your wallet!

Knock knock!
Who's there?
Cyprus!
Cyprus who?
Cyprus the bell!

Knock knock!
Who's there?
Yo mama!
Yo mama who?
Seriously, this is your mother. Open the door or you are grounded!

Knock knock!
Who's there?
Brent!
Brent who?
Brent out of shape!

Knock knock!
Who's there?
Brad!
Brad who?
I have Brad new I'm afraid!

Knock knock!
Who's there?
Burns!
Burns who?
Burns me up!

Knock knock!
Who's there?
Bug!
Bug who?
You are bugging me!

Knock knock!
Who's there?
Button!
Button who?
Button in is not a polite thing to do!

Knock knock!
Who's there?
Cheese!
Cheese who?
Cheese a jolly good fellow!

Knock knock!
Who's there?
Boris!
Boris who?
Please don't Boris with more knock knock jokes!

Knock knock!
Who's there?
Bologna!
Bologna who?
Bologna and cheese please!

Knock knock!
Who's there?
Moo!
Moo who?
Are you a cow or an owl?

Knock knock!
Who's there?
Boliva!
Boliva who?
Boliva me, I know what I'm talking about!

Knock knock!
Who's there?
Cynthia!
Cynthia who?
Cynthia been away I missed you!

Knock knock!
Who's there?
Checkmate!
Checkmate who?
Checkmate bounce if you don't have enough money in the bank!

Knock knock!
Who's there?
Chicken!
Chicken who?
Chicken your pockets. I think your keys are there!

Knock knock!
Who's there?
Chile!
Chile who?
Chile out tonight!

Knock knock!
Who's there?
Tex!
Tex who?
It Tex two to tango!

Knock knock!
Who's there?
Wade!
Wade who?
Wade up! I am behind!

Knock knock!
Who's there?
Chips!
Chips who?
Chips ahoy!

Knock knock!
Who's there?
Carrie!
Carrie who?
Carrie my bag!

Knock knock!
Who's there?
Water!
Water who?
Water you doing this weekend?

Knock knock!
Who's there?
Cat!
Cat who?
Cat you understand anything!

Knock knock!
Who's there?
Cash!
Cash who?
Cash me if you can!

Knock knock!
Who's there?
Argue!
Argue who?
Argue going to let me in the house?

Knock knock!
Who's there?
Catskill!
Catskill who?
Catskill mice!

Knock knock!
Who's there?
Chair!
Chair who?
Chair you go again, asking more questions!

Knock knock!
Who's there?
Celeste!
Celeste who?
Celeste time I lend you money!

Knock knock!
Who's there?
Cam!
Cam who?
Camalot is where King Arthur lived!

Knock knock!
Who's there?
Ben!
Ben who?
Ben away for too long!

Knock knock!
Who's there?
Caesar!
Caesar who?
Caesar quickly before she gets away!

Knock knock!
Who's there?
Tank!
Tank who?
You are welcome!

Knock knock!
Who's there?
Candice!
Candice who?
Candice get any better?

Knock knock!
Who's there?
A little boy!
A little boy who?
A little boy that can't reach the door knob!

Knock knock!
Who's there?
Candy!
Candy who?
Candy cow jump over the moon?

Knock knock!
Who's there?
Cargo!
Cargo who?
Cargo better if you fill it up with gas first!

Knock knock!
Who's there?
Ear!
Ear who?
Ear you are. I've been looking for you!

Knock knock!
Who's there?
Bunny!
Bunny who?
The bunny thing is that I've forgotten now!

Knock knock!
Who's there?
Cameron!
Cameron who?
Cameron film are needed to take pictures!

Knock knock!
Who's there?
Geno!
Geno who?
Geno any good jokes?

Knock knock!
Who's there?
Cantaloupe!
Cantaloupe who?
Cantaloupe with you tonight!

Knock knock!
Who's there?
Earl!
Earl who?
Earl be glad when you finally open the door!

Knock knock!
Who's there?
Cannelloni!
Cannelloni who?
Cannelloni some money until next week?

Knock knock!
Who's there?
Byron!
Byron who?
Byron some new clothes!

Knock knock!
Who's there?
Rain!
Rain who?
Rain deer. The same ones that lead Santa's sleigh.

Knock knock!
Who's there?
Callas!
Callas who?
Callas should be removed by a podiatrist!

Knock knock!
Who's there?
It's Sam.
It's Sam who?
It's Sam person that knocked on the door earlier!

Knock knock!
Who's there?
Cain!
Cain who?
Cain you tell? It's me!

Knock knock!
Who's there?
Butch!
Butch who?
Butch your arms around me!

Knock knock!
Who's there?
Jade!
Jade who?
Jade an entire birthday cake this morning!

Knock knock!
Who's there?
Buster!
Buster who?
Buster tire, can I use your phone?

Knock knock!
Who's there?
China!
China who?
China late, isn't it?

Knock knock!
Who's there?
Ten!
Ten who?
Ten to your own business!

Knock knock!
Who's there?
Bush!
Bush who?
Bush your money where your mouth is!

Knock knock!
Who's there?
Two!
Two who?
Two be or not two be? That is the question.

Knock knock!
Who's there?
Burton!
Burton who?
Burton in the hand is worth two in the bush!

Knock knock!
Who's there?
Cherry!
Cherry who?
Cherry oh, see you later!

Knock knock!
Who's there?
Tuna!
Tuna who?
Tuna guitar and it will sound much better!

Knock knock!
Who's there?
Bully!
Bully who?
Bully Jean is not my lover!

Knock knock!
Who's there?
Sarah!
Sarah who?
Sarah other way in?

Knock knock!
Who's there?
Bullet!
Bullet who?
Bullet all the hay and now he's hungry again!

Knock knock!
Who's there?
Castro!
Castro who?
Castro bread upon the waters!

Knock knock!
Who's there?
Bruno!
Bruno who?
Bruno more tea for me!

Knock knock!
Who's there?
Bruce!
Bruce who?
I Bruce very easily. Please don't hit me!

Knock knock!
Who's there?
Census!
Census who?
Census lots of presents for Christmas!

Knock knock!
Who's there?
Cassie!
Cassie who?
Cassie the forest for all the trees!

Knock knock!
Who's there?
Beef!
Beef who?
Beef fair now!

Knock knock!
Who's there?
Jess.
Jess who?
Jess the way it is!

Knock knock!
Who's there?
Czech!
Czech who?
Czech before you open the door!

Knock knock!
Who's there?
Brie!
Brie who?
Brie me my supper!

Knock knock!
Who's there?
Egg.
Egg who?
It's eggstremely cold out here. Open up!

Knock knock!
Who's there?
Bridget!
Bridget who?
London Bridget falling down, falling down!

Knock knock!
Who's there?
Bones!
Bones who?
Bones upon a time!

Knock knock!
Who's there?
Candace!
Candace who?
Candace with love!

Knock knock!
Who's there!
Bond!
Bond who?
Bond to succeed!

Knock knock!
Who's there?
Scold!
Scold who?
Scold out here. Let me in!

Knock knock!
Who's there?
Boise!
Boise who?
Boise ivy!

Knock knock!
Who's there?
Carrie!
Carrie who?
Carrie me home, I'm tired!

Knock knock!
Who's there?
Boiler!
Boiler who?
Boiler egg for 4-5 minutes!

Knock knock!
Who's there?
Bless!
Bless who?
I didn't sneeze!

Knock knock!
Who's there?
Cartoon!
Cartoon who?
Cartoon up just fine. She purrs just like a cat!

Knock knock!
Who's there?
Bun!
Bun who?
Bun-nies make great pets!

Knock knock!
Who's there?
Read!
Read who?
Read between the lines!

Knock knock!
Who's there?
Camilla!
Camilla who?
Camilla minute!

Knock knock!
Who's there?
Gluck!
Gluck who?
Gluck for a spare key for me to have!

Knock knock!
Who's there?
Caroline!
Caroline who?
Caroline of rope with you!

Knock knock!
Who's there?
Bjorn!
Bjorn who?
Bjorn with a silver spoon in his mouth!

Knock knock!
Who's there?
Biro!
Biro who?
Biro light of the moon!

Knock knock!
Who's there?
Razor.
Razor who?
Razor hands, this is a stick-up!

Knock knock!
Who's there?
Edwin!
Edwin who?
Edwin some and you lose some!

Knock knock!
Who's there?
Shelby!
Shelby who?
Shelby coming around the mountain when she comes!

ABOUT THE AUTHOR

The Joke King, Johnny B. Laughing is a best-selling children's joke book author. He is a jokester at heart and enjoys a good laugh, pulling pranks on his friends, and telling funny and hilarious jokes!

For more funny joke books just search for *JOHNNY B. LAUGHING* on Amazon.com

Visit the website:
www.funny-jokes-online.weebly.com

Made in the USA
Coppell, TX
23 December 2021